A FIRST GOLDEN TREASURY
OF
ANIMAL
VERSE

COMPILED BY MARK DANIEL

M

MACMILLAN CHILDREN'S BOOKS

For Ann

A First Golden Treasury of Animal Verse

Conceived by Breslich & Foss
This anthology copyright © Breslich & Foss
Designed by Roger Daniels

First published in Great Britain in 1986 by Pavilion Books Limited
in association with Michael Joseph Limited

Premier Picturemac edition published 1991 by
Macmillan Children's Books
A division of Macmillan Publishers Limited
London and Basingstoke
Associated companies throughout the world

ISBN 0–333–55191–5

A CIP catalogue record for this book is available from the British Library

Printed in Hong Kong

All colour pictures are courtesy of
Fine Art Photographic Library, London

Front cover painting by Arthur Herbert Buckland (1870–1927)
Back cover painting by Paolo Sala (1859–1929)

Poems by Hilaire Belloc which appear in this
anthology are reprinted by kind permission of
Peters, Fraser & Dunlop Group Ltd

CONTENTS

MAN'S BEST FRIENDS

Pussy can sit by the fire and sing,
   Pussy can climb a tree,
Or play with a silly old cork and string
To 'muse herself, not me.
But I like Binkie my dog, because
He knows how to behave;
So, Binkie's the same as the first Friend was,
And I am the Man in the Cave.

Pussy will play Man-Friday till
It's time to wet her paw
And make her walk on the window-sill
(For the footprint Crusoe saw);
Then she fluffles her tail and mews,
And scratches and won't attend.
But Binkie will play whenever I choose,
And he is my true first friend.

Pussy will rub my knees with her head
Pretending she loves me hard;
But the very minute I go to bed
Pussy runs out in the yard,
And there she stays till the morning-light;
So I know it is only pretend;
But Binkie, he snores at my feet all night,
And he is my Firstest Friend!

RUDYARD KIPLING
Just So Stories, 1902

My dog's so furry I've not seen
His face for years and years:
His eyes are buried out of sight,
I only guess his ears.

When people ask me for his breed,
I do not know or care:
He has the beauty of them all
Hidden beneath his hair.

HERBERT ASQUITH

HURT NO LIVING THING

Hurt no living thing,
Ladybird nor butterfly,
Nor moth with dusty wing,
Nor cricket chirping cheerily,
Nor grasshopper, so light of leap,
Nor dancing gnat,
Nor beetle fat,
Nor harmless worms that creep.

CHRISTINA ROSSETTI
Sing-Song, 1872

THE CAT AND THE MOON

The cat went here and there
   And the moon spun round like a top,
And the nearest kin of the moon,
The creeping cat, looked up.
Black Minnaloushe stared at the moon,
For, wander and wail as he would,
The pure cold light in the sky
Troubled his animal blood.
Minnaloushe runs in the grass
Lifting his delicate feet.
Do you dance, Minnaloushe, do you dance?
When two close kindred meet,
What better than call a dance?
Maybe the moon may learn,
Tired of that courtly fashion,
A new dance turn.
Minnaloushe creeps through the grass
From moonlit place to place,
The sacred moon overhead
Has taken a new phase.
Does Minnaloushe know that his pupils
Will pass from change to change,
And that from round to crescent,
From crescent to round they range?
Minnaloushe creeps through the grass
Alone, important and wise,
And lifts to the changing moon
His changing eyes.

W. B. YEATS
The Wild Swans at Coole, 1919

OLD MOTHER HUBBARD

Old Mother Hubbard
Went to the cupboard
To get her poor dog a bone,
But when she got there
The cupboard was bare
And so the poor dog had none.

She went to the baker's
To buy him some bread,
But when she came back
The poor dog was dead.

She went to the joiner's
To buy him a coffin,
But when she came back
The poor dog was laughing.

She took a clean dish
To get him some tripe,
But when she came back
He was smoking his pipe.

She went to the fish-man's
To buy him some fish,
And when she came back
He was licking the dish.

She went to the ale-house
To get him some beer,
But when she came back
The dog sat in a chair.

She went to the tavern
For white wine and red,
But when she came back
The dog stood on his head.

She went to the hatter's
To buy him a hat,
But when she came back
He was feeding the cat.

She went to the barber's
To buy him a wig,
But when she came back
He was dancing a jig.

She went to the tailor's
To buy him a coat,
But when she came back
He was riding a goat.

She went to the cobbler's
To buy him some shoes,
But when she came back
He was reading the news.

She went to the seamstress
To buy him some linen,
But when she came back
The dog was spinning.

She went to the hosier's
To buy him some hose,
But when she came back
He was dressed in his clothes.

The dame made a curtsy,
The dog made a bow;
The dame said, "Your servant,"
The dog said, "Bow wow."

ANON

THE KITTEN PLAYING
WITH THE FALLING LEAVES

See the kitten on the wall
Sporting with the leaves that fall!
Withered leaves, one, two, and three,
From the lofty elder-tree.
Through the calm and frosty air
Of this morning bright and fair
Eddying round and round they sink
Softly, slowly. — One might think,
From the motions that are made,
Every little leaf conveyed
Some small fairy, hither tending,
To this lower world descending.
—But the kitten how she starts!
Crouches, stretches, paws, and darts:
First at one, and then its fellow,
Just as light, and just as yellow:
There are many now — now one —
Now they stop and there are none.
What intentness of desire
In her up-turned eye of fire!
With a tiger-leap half way,
Now she meets the coming prey.
Lets it go at last, and then
Has it in her power again.

WILLIAM WORDSWORTH

W ho's that ringing at the front door bell?"
Miau! Miau! Miau!
"I'm a little Pussy Cat and I'm not very well!"
Miau! Miau! Miau!
"Then rub your nose in a bit of mutton fat."
Miau! Miau! Miau!
"For that's the way to cure a little Pussy Cat."
Miau! Miau! Miau!

D'ARCY WENTWORTH THOMPSON
Nursery Nonsense, 1864

THE PEKINESE

The Pekinese
  Adore their ease
And slumber like the dead;
In comfort curled
They view the world
As one unending bed.

E. V. LUCAS

There was a little dog, and he had a little tail,
  And he used to wag, wag, wag it.
But whenever he was sad because he had been bad,
On the ground he would drag, drag, drag it.

He had a little nose, as of course you would suppose,
And on it was a muz-muz-muzzle,
And to get it off he'd try till a tear stood in his eye,
But he found it a puz-puz-puzzle.

ANON

There was a man, and his name was Dob,
  And he had a wife, and her name was Mob,
And he had a dog, and he called it Cob,
And she had a cat called Chitterabob.

"Cob!," calls Dob.
"Chitterabob!," calls Mob.
Cob was Dob's dog.
Chitterabob Mob's cat.

ANON

HIS APOLOGIES

Master, this is Thy Servant. He is rising eight
     weeks old.
He is mainly Head and Tummy. His legs are
     uncontrolled.
But Thou hast forgiven his ugliness, and settled him
     on thy knee...
Art Thou content with Thy Servant? He is *very*
     comfy with Thee.

Master, behold a Sinner? He hath done grievous
     wrong.
He hath defiled Thy Premises through being kept in
     too long.
Wherefore his nose has been rubbed in the dirt, and
     his self-respect has been bruised.
Master, pardon Thy Sinner, and see he is properly
     loosed.

Master — again Thy Sinner! This that was once Thy
     Shoe,
He hath found and taken and carried aside, as fitting
     matter to chew.
Now there is neither blacking nor tongue, and the
     Housemaid has us in toe.
Master, remember Thy Servant is young,
     and tell her to let him go!

Master, behold Thy Servant! Strange children came
    to play
And because they fought to caress him, Thy Servant
    wentedst away.
But now that the Little Beasts have gone, he has
    returned to see
(Brushed — with his Sunday collar on —) what they
    left over from tea.

Master, pity Thy Servant! He is deaf and three parts
    blind,
He cannot catch Thy Commandments. He cannot
    read Thy Mind.
Oh, leave him not in his loneliness; nor make him
    that kitten's scorn.
He has had none other God than Thee since the year
    that he was born!

Lord, look down on Thy Servant! Bad things have
    come to pass,
There is no heat in the midday sun nor health in the
    wayside grass.
His bones are full of an old disease — his torments
    run and increase.
Lord, make haste with Thy Lightnings, and grant
    him a quick release!

RUDYARD KIPLING
Thy Servant A Dog, 1930.

21

Pussy cat sits by the fire;
   How did she come there?
In walks the little dog,
Says, "Pussy! Are you there?"

"How do you do, Mistress Pussy?
Mistress Pussy, how d'ye do?"
"I thank you kindly, little dog,
I fare as well as you!"

ANON

CATS OF KILKENNY

There once were two cats of Kilkenny;
  Each thought there was one cat too many;
So they fought and they fit,
And they scratched and they bit,
Till, excepting their nails
And the tips of their tails,
Instead of two cats, there weren't any.

ANON

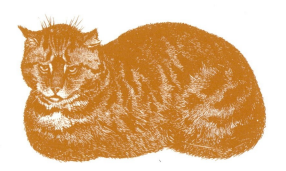

THE CAT OF CATS

I am the cat of cats. I am
The everlasting cat!
Cunning, and old, and sleek as jam,
The everlasting cat!
I hunt the vermin in the night —
The everlasting cat!
For I see best without the light —
The everlasting cat!

WILLIAM BRIGHTY RANDS
Good Words for the Young, 1868

Dame Trot and her cat
  Sat down for to chat;
The Dame sat on this side,
And Puss sat on that.

"Puss," says the Dame,
"Can you catch a rat,
Or a mouse in the dark?"
"Purr," says the cat.

ANON

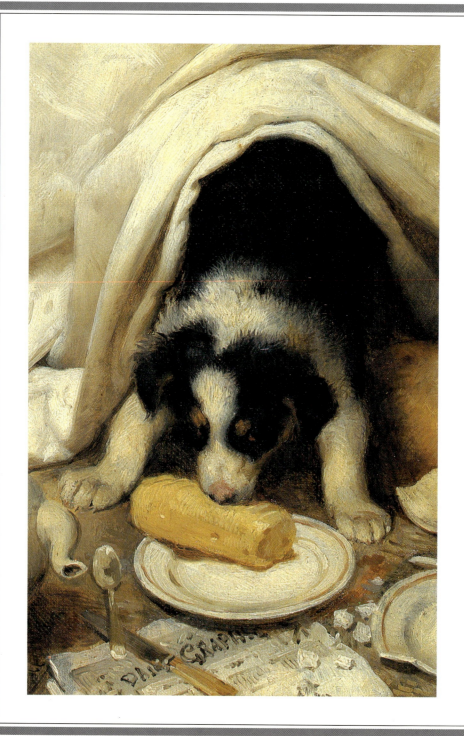

THE DINERS
IN THE KITCHEN

Our dog Fred
Et the bread

Our dog Dash
Et the hash

Our dog Pete
Et the meat

Our dog Davy
Et the gravy

Our dog Toffy
Et the coffee

Our dog Jake
Et the cake

Our dog Trip
Et the dip

And — the worst,
From the first —

Our dog Fido
Et the pie-dough

JAMES WHITCOMB RILEY
Rhymes of Childhood, 1891

ALL CREATURES GREAT...

THE ELEPHANT

Here comes the elephant
Swaying along
With his cargo of children
All singing a song:
To the tinkle of laughter
He goes on his way,
And his cargo of children
Have crowned him with may.

His legs are in leather
And padded his toes;
He can root up an oak
With a whisk of his nose;
With a wave of his trunk
And a turn of his chin
He can pull down a house,
Or pick up a pin.
Beneath his grey forehead
A little eye peers;
Of what is he thinking
Between those wide ears?
What does he feel?

If he wished to tease,
He could twirl his keeper
Over the trees;
If he were not kind,
He could play cup and ball
With Robert and Helen,
And Uncle Paul;

But that grey forehead,
Those crinkled ears,
Have learned to be kind
In a hundred years:
And so with the children
He goes on his way
To the tinkle of laughter
And crowned with the may.

HERBERT ASQUITH

THE CAMEL'S LAMENT

Canary-birds feed on sugar and seed,
  Parrots have crackers to crunch;
And as for the poodles, they tell me the noodles
Have chickens and cream for their lunch.
  But there's never a question
  About MY digestion —
Anything does for me!

"Cats, you're aware, can repose in a chair,
  Chickens can roost upon rails;
Puppies are able to sleep in a stable,
And oysters can slumber in pails.
  But no one supposes
  A poor Camel dozes —
Any place does for me!

"Lambs are enclosed where it's never exposed.
Coops are constructed for hens;
Kittens are treated to houses well heated,
And pigs are protected by pens.
But a Camel comes handy
Wherever it's sandy —
Anywhere does for me!

"People would laugh if you rode a giraffe,
Or mounted the back of an ox;
It's nobody's habit to ride on a rabbit,
Or try to bestraddle a fox.
But as for a Camel, he's
Ridden by families —
Any load does for me!

"A snake is as round as a hole in the ground,
And weasels are wavy and sleek;
And no alligator could ever be straighter
Than lizards that live in a creek.
But a Camel's all lumpy
And bumpy and humpy —
ANY shape does for me!"

CHARLES EDWARD CARRYL
The Admiral's Caravan, 1892

THE PELICAN CHORUS

King and Queen of the Pelicans we;
No other Birds so grand we see!
None but we have feet like fins!
With lovely leathery throats and chins!
  Ploffskin, Pluffskin, Pelican jee!
  We think no Birds so happy as we!
  Plumpskin, Ploshkin, Pelican jill!
  We think so then, and we thought so still!

We live on the Nile. The Nile we love.
By night we sleep on cliffs above;
By day we fish, and at eve we stand
On long bare islands of yellow sand.
And when the sun sinks slowly down
And the great rockwalls grow dark and brown
And the purple river rolls fast and dim,
And the ivory Ibis starlike skim,
Wing to wing we dance around –
Stamping our feet with a flumpy sound, –
Opening our mouths as Pelicans ought,
And this is the song we nightly snort;
  Ploffskin, Pluffskin, Pelican jee! —
  We think no Birds so happy as we!
  Plumpskin, Ploshkin, Pelican jill!
  We think so then, and we thought so still!

EDWARD LEAR
Laughable Lyrics, 1877

THE CROCODILE

How doth the little crocodile
Improve his shining tail
And pour the waters of the Nile
On every golden scale!

How cheerfully he seems to grin,
How neatly spreads his claws,
And welcomes little fishes in
With gently smiling jaws!

LEWIS CARROLL
Alice's Adventures in Wonderland, 1865

If you should meet a crocodile,
Don't take a stick and poke him;
Ignore the welcome of his smile,
Be careful not to stroke him.
For as he sleeps upon the Nile,
He thinner gets and thinner;
And where'er you meet a crocodile,
He's ready for his dinner.

ANON

THE LION

The Lion, the Lion, he dwells in the waste,
  He has a big head and a very small waist;
But his shoulders are stark, and his jaws they are
  grim,
And a good little child will not play with him.

HILAIRE BELLOC
The Bad Child's Book of Beasts, 1896

THE YAK

As a friend to the children, commend me the yak;
You will find it exactly the thing:
It will carry and fetch, you can ride on its back,
Or lead it about with a string.

The Tartar who dwells in the plains of Tibet
(A desolate region of snow),
Has for centuries made it a nursery pet,
And surely the Tartar should know!

Then tell your papa where the yak can be got,
And if he is awfully rich,
He will buy you the creature — or else he will not:
I cannot be positive which.

HILAIRE BELLOC
A Bad Child's Book of Beasts, 1896

I asked my mother for fifty cents
To see the elephant jump the fence.
He jumped so high he touched the sky
And never came back till the Fourth of July.

ANON

THE NYMPH AND HER FAWN

With sweetest milk and sugar first
I it at my own fingers nursed;
And as it grew, so every day
It wax'd more white and sweet than they —
It had so sweet a breath! and oft
I blush'd to see its foot more soft
And white — shall I say? — than my hand,
Nay, any lady's of the land!

It is a wondrous thing how fleet
'Twas on those little silver feet:
With what a pretty skipping grace
It oft would challenge me the race: —
And when't had left me far away
'Twould stay, and run again, and stay:
For it was nimbler much than hinds,
And trod as if on the four winds.

ANDREW MARVELL
Miscellaneous Poems, 1681

Hast thou given the horse strength? hast thou
clothed his neck with thunder?
Canst thou make him afraid as a grasshopper?
  The glory of his nostrils *is* terrible.
He paweth in the valley, and rejoiceth in *his* strength:
  he goeth on to meet the armed men.
He mocketh at fear, and is not affrighted; neither
  turneth he back from the sword.
The quiver rattleth against him, the glittering spear
  and the shield.
He swalloweth the ground with fierceness and rage:
  neither believeth he that *it is* the sound of the
  trumpet.
He saith among the trumpets, Ha, ha; and he
  smelleth the battle afar off, the thunder of the
  captains, and the shouting.

JOB, CHAPTER 39, Verses 19-25

AT THE ZOO

First I saw the white bear, then I saw the black;
Then I saw the camel with a hump upon his back;
Then I saw the grey wolf, with mutton in his maw;
Then I saw the wombat waddle in the straw;
Then I saw the elephant a-waving of his trunk;
Then I saw the monkeys — mercy, how unpleasantly
  they — smelt!

WILLIAM MAKEPEACE THACKERAY
Works, 1879

Fuzzy Wuzzy was a bear,
A bear was Fuzzy Wuzzy.
When Fuzzy Wuzzy lost his hair
He wasn't fuzzy, was he?

ANON

SEAL LULLABY

Oh, hush thee, my baby, the night is behind us,
    And black are the waters that sparkled so green
The moon o'er the combers, looks downward to
    find us
At rest in the hollows that rustle between.
Where billow meets billow, there soft be thy pillow;
Ah, weary wee flipperling, curl at thy ease!
The storm shall not wake thee, nor sharks overtake
    thee,
Asleep in the arms of the slow-swinging sea.

RUDYARD KIPLING
The Jungle Books, 1914

THE TYGER

Tyger! Tyger! burning bright
In the forests of the night,
What immortal hand or eye
Could frame thy fearful symmetry?

In what distant deeps or skies
Burnt the fire of thine eyes?
On what wings dare he aspire?
What the hand dare seize the fire?

And what shoulder, and what art,
Could twist the sinews of thy heart?
And when thy heart began to beat,
What dread hand? and what dread feet?

What the hammer? what the chain?
In what furnace was thy brain?
What the anvil? what dread grasp
Dare its deadly terrors clasp?

When the stars threw down their spears,
And watered Heaven with their tears,
Did he smile his work to see?
Did He who made the Lamb make thee?

Tyger! Tyger! burning bright
In the forests of the night,
What immortal hand or eye,
Dare frame thy fearful symmetry?

WILLIAM BLAKE
Songs of Experience, 1794

THE FLY-AWAY HORSE

Oh, a wonderful horse is the Fly-Away Horse —
Perhaps you have seen him before;
Perhaps, while you slept, his shadow has swept
Through the moonlight that floats on the floor.
For it's only at night, when the stars twinkle bright,
That the Fly-Away Horse, with a neigh
And a pull at his rein and a toss of his mane,
Is up on his heels and away!
The Moon in the sky,
As he gallopeth by,
Cries: "Oh! what a marvellous sight!"
And the Stars in dismay
Hide their faces away
In the lap of old Grandmother Night.

Off! scamper to bed — you shall ride him to-night!
For, as soon as you've fallen asleep,
With a jubilant neigh he shall bear you away
Over forest and hillside and deep!
But tell us, my dear, all you see and you hear
In those beautiful lands over there,
Where the Fly-Away Horse wings his far-away
    course
With the wee one consigned to his care.
Then grandma will cry
In amazement: "Oh, my!"
And she'll think it could never be so.
And only we two
Shall know it is true —
You and I, little precious! shall know!

EUGENE FIELD
excerpt, Poems of Childhood, 1892

THE DONKEY

When fishes flew and forests walked
  And figs grew upon the thorn
Some moment when the moon was blood
Then surely I was born.

With monstrous head and sickening cry
And ears like errant wings,
The devil's walking parody
On all four-footed things.

The tattered outlaw of the earth,
Of ancient crooked will;
Starve, scourge, deride me; I am dumb,
I keep my secret still.

Fools! For I also had my hour;
One far fierce hour and sweet:
There was a shout about my ears,
And palms before my feet.

G. K. CHESTERTON
The Wild Knight, 1900

FALLOW DEER

One without looks in tonight
Through the curtain chink
From the sheet of glistening white;
One without looks in tonight
As we sit and think
By the fender-brink.

We do not discern those eyes
Watching in the snow;
Lit by lamps of rosy dyes
We do not discern those eyes
Wondering, aglow,
Fourfooted, tiptoe.

THOMAS HARDY
Late Lyrics, 1922

The lion and the unicorn
  Were fighting for the crown;
The lion beat the unicorn
All round the town.
Some gave them white bread,
And some gave them brown;
Some gave them plum cake,
And sent them out of town.

ANON

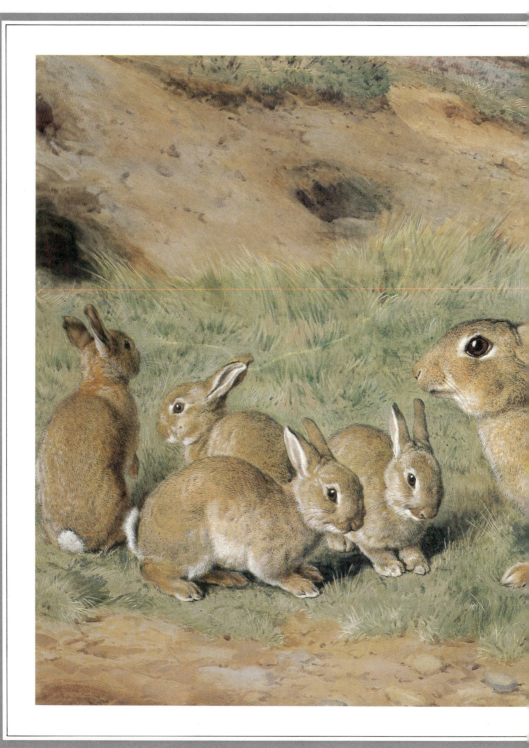

...And Small

A cat came fiddling out of a barn,
With a pair of bagpipes under her arm,
She could sing nothing but "Fiddle-de-de.
The mouse has married the bumblebee."
Pipe, cat — dance, mouse —
We'll have a wedding at our good house.

ANON

TO A SQUIRREL

Come play with me
Why should you run
Through the shaking tree
As though I'd a gun
To strike you dead?
When all I would do
Is to scratch your head
And let you go.

W. B. YEATS
The Wild Swans at Coole, 1919

THE FROG

Be kind and tender to the frog,
And do not call him names,
As "Slimy-Skin" or "Pollywog,"
Or likewise "Uncle James,"
Or "Gape-a-grin," or "Toad-gone-wrong,"
Or "Billy Bandy-Knees;"
The frog is justly sensitive
To epithets like these.

No animal will more repay
A treatment kind and fair,
At least, so lonely people say
Who keep a frog (and by the way,
They are extremely rare).

HILAIRE BELLOC
A Bad Child's Book of Beasts, 1896

THREE MICE

Three little mice walked into town,
  Their coats were grey, and their eyes were
brown.

Three little mice went down the street,
With woolwork slippers upon their feet.

Three little mice sat down to dine
On curranty bread and gooseberry wine.

Three little mice ate on and on,
Till every crumb of the bread was gone.

Three little mice, when the feast was done,
Crept home quietly one by one.

Three little mice went straight to bed,
And dreamt of crumbly, curranty bread.

CHARLOTTE DRUITT COLE

SNAKE

A narrow fellow in the grass
Occasionally rides;
You may have met him — did you not?
His notice sudden is.

The grass divides as with a comb,
A spotted shaft is seen,
And then it closes at your feet
And opens further on.

He likes a boggy acre,
A floor too cool for corn;
Yet when a child and barefoot,
I more than once at noon

Have passed, I thought, a whiplash
Upbraiding in the sun;
When, stooping to secure it,
It wrinkled and was gone.

Several of nature's people
I know, and they know me;
I feel for them a transport
Of cordiality

But never met this fellow,
Attended or alone,
Without a tighter breathing
And zero at the bone.

EMILY DICKINSON
Poems, 1890

THE SILENT SNAKE

The birds go fluttering in the air,
  The rabbits run and skip,
Brown squirrels race along the bough,
The May-flies rise and dip;
But, whilst these creatures play and leap,
The silent snake goes creepy-creep!

The birdies sing and whistle loud,
The busy insects hum,
The squirrels chat, the frogs say "croak!"
But the snake is always dumb.
With not a sound through grasses deep
The silent snake goes creepy-creep!

ANON

WE FISH

We fish, we fish, we merrily swim,
  We care not for friend nor for foe.
Our fins are stout,
Our tails are out,
As through the seas we go.

Fish, fish, we are fish with red gills;
Naught disturbs us, our blood is at zero:
We are buoyant because of our bags,
Being many, each fish is a hero.
We care not what is it, this life

That we follow, this phantom unknown;
To swim, it's exceedingly pleasant —
So swim away, making a foam.
This strange looking thing by our side,
Not for safety, around it we flee: —
Its shadow's so shady, that's all —
We only swim under its lee.
And as for the eels there above,
And as for the fowls of the air,
We care not for them nor their ways,
As we cheerily glide afar!

HERMAN MELVILLE
Mardi, 1849.

Little Tim Sprat
Had a pet rat,
In a tin cage with a wheel.
Said little Tim Sprat,
Each day to his rat:
"If hungry, my dear, you must squeal."

ANON

Croak!" said the Toad, "I'm hungry, I think;
Today I've had nothing to eat or to drink;
I'll crawl to a garden and jump through the pales,
And there I'll dine nicely on slugs and on snails."
"Ho, ho!" quoth the Frog, "is that what you mean?
Then I'll hop away to the next meadow stream;
There I will drink, and eat worms and slugs too,
And then I shall have a good dinner like you."

ANON

SIX LITTLE MICE

Six little mice sat down to spin;
Pussy passed by and she peeped in.
"What are you doing, my little men?"
"Weaving coats for gentlemen."
"Shall I come in and cut off your threads?"
"Oh, no, Mistress Pussy, you'd bite off our heads!"

ANON

THE MOUNTAIN AND
THE SQUIRREL

The mountain and the squirrel
  Had a quarrel;
And the former called the latter "Little Prig."
Bun replied,
"You are doubtless very big;
But all sorts of things and weather
Must be taken in together,
To make up a year
And a sphere.
And I think it no disgrace
To occupy my place.
If I'm not so large as you,
You are not so small as I,
And not half so spry,
I'll not deny you make
A very pretty squirrel track;
Talents differ; all is well and wisely put;
If I cannot carry forests on my back,
Neither can you crack a nut."

RALPH WALDO EMERSON
Poems, 1914

FINGER PLAY

This little bunny said, "Let's play."
This little bunny said, "In the hay."
This one saw a man with a gun.
This one said, "This isn't fun."
This one said, "I'm off for a run."
Bang! went the gun,
They ran away
And didn't come back for a year and a day.

ANON

THE SQUIRREL

The squirrel, flippant, pert and full of play,
   Drawn from his refuge in some lonely elm
That age or injury hath hollowed deep,
Where, on his bed of wool and matted leaves,
He has out-slept the winter, ventures forth
To frisk awhile, and bask in the warm sun:
He sees me, and at once, swift as a bird,
Ascends the neighbouring beech: there whisks his
   brush,
And perks his ears, and stamps, and cries aloud,
With all the prettiness of feigned alarm,
And anger insignificantly fierce.

WILLIAM COWPER
Works, 1905

TWO RATS

He was a rat, and she was a rat
And down in one hole they did dwell,
And both were as black as a witch's cat
And they loved one another well.

He had a tail, and she had a tail
Both long and curling and fine;
And each said, "Yours is the finest tail
In the world — excepting mine."

He smelled the cheese, and she smelled the cheese,
And they both pronounced it good;
And both remarked it would greatly add
To the charms of their daily food.

So he ventured out, and she ventured out,
And I saw them go with pain,
But what befell them I never can tell
For they never came back again.

ANON

A LOBSTER QUADRILLE

Will you walk a little faster?" said a whiting to
    a snail,
"There's a porpoise close behind us, and he's treading
    on my tail
See how eagerly the lobsters and the turtles
    all advance!
They are waiting on the shingle — will you come
    and join the dance?
Will you, won't you, will you, won't you, will you
    join the dance?
Will you, won't you, will you, won't you, will you
    join the dance?
You can really have no notion how delightful it
    will be
When they take us up and throw us, with the
    lobsters, out to sea!"
But the snail replied, "Too far, too far!" and gave
    a look askance —

Said he thanked the whiting kindly, but he would
    not join the dance.
Would not, could not, would not, could not, could
    not join the dance.
Would not, could not, would not, could not, could
    not join the dance.
"What matters it how far we go?" his scaly friend
    replied,
"There is another shore, you know, upon the other
    side.
The further off from England, the nearer is to
    France —
Then turn not pale, beloved snail, but come and join
    the dance.
Will, you, won't you, will you, won't you, will you
    join the dance?
Will you, won't you, will you, won't you, will you
    join the dance?"

LEWIS CARROLL
Alice's Adventures in Wonderland, 1865

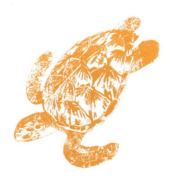

WHISKY FRISKY

Whisky, frisky,
  Hipperty hop,
Up he goes
To the tree top!

Whirly, twirly,
Round and round,
Down he scampers
To the ground.

Furly, curly,
What a tail,
Tall as a feather,
Broad as a sail.

Where's his supper?
In the shell.
Snappy, cracky,
Out it fell.

ANON

THE SQUIRREL

The winds they did blow,
  The leaves they did wag;
Along came a beggar boy
And put me in his bag.
He took me to London;
A lady did me buy,
And put me in a silver cage,
And hung me up on high;
With apples by the fire,
And hazelnuts to crack,
Besides a little feather bed
To rest my tiny back.

ANON

A FRIEND IN THE GARDEN

He is not John the gardener,
   And yet the whole day long
Employs himself most usefully,
The flower beds among.

He is not Tom the pussy cat,
And yet the other day,
With stealthy stride and glistening eye,
He crept upon his prey.

He is not Dash the dear old dog,
And yet, perhaps, if you
Took pains with him and petted him,
You'd come to love him too.

He's not a blackbird, though he chirps,
And though he once was black;
And now he wears a loose grey coat,
All wrinkled on the back.

He's got a very dirty face,
And very shining eyes;
He sometimes comes and sits indoors;
He looks — and p'r'aps is — wise.

But in a sunny flower bed
He has a fixed abode;
He eats the things that eat my plants —
He is a friendly TOAD.

JULIANA HORATIA EWING
Aunt Judy's Magazine, 1873

FROG WENT A-COURTIN'

Mr. Froggie went a-courtin' an' he did ride;
Sword and pistol by his side.

He went to Missus Mousie's hall,
Gave a loud knock and gave a loud call.

"Pray, Missus Mousie, air you within?"
"Yes, kind sir, I set an' spin."

He tuk Miss Mousie on his knee,
An' sez, "Miss Mousie, will ya marry me?"

Miss Mousie blushed an' hung her head,
"You'll have t'ask Uncle Rat," she said.

"Not without Uncle Rat's consent
Would I marry the Pres-i-dent."

Uncle Rat jumped up an' shuck his fat side,
To think his niece would be Bill Frog's bride.

Nex' day Uncle Rat went to town,
To git his niece a weddin' gown.

Whar shall the weddin' supper be?
'Way down yander in a holler tree.

First come in was a Bumble-bee,
Who danced a jig with Captain Flea.

Next come in was a Butterfly,
Sellin' butter very high.

An' when they all set down to sup,
A big gray goose come an' gobbled 'em all up.

An' this is the end of one, two, three,
The Rat an' the Mouse an' the little Froggie.

ANON

THE POETS

BELLOC, Joseph Hilaire Pierre
(1870–1953) France
Historian, poet, essayist, novelist, and
traveller. Belloc was born near Paris, but was
forced to flee with his mother to England by
the Franco-Prussian war. An astoundingly
prolific author, his more celebrated works
include *A Bad Child's Book of Beasts* (1896) and
More Beasts (1897), from which the verses in
this collection are taken; *Danton* (1899); *The
Path to Rome* (1902); *Cautionary Tales for Children*
(1907); *The French Revolution* (1911); and *The
Cruise of "the Nona"* (1925). A devout Catholic
and a great friend of G.K. Chesterton (q.v.),
he left an enormous legacy of works
characterized by intellectual vigor, euphony,
contentiousness, and down-to-earth
spirituality.

BLAKE, William
(1757–1827) UK
Poet, painter, and visionary, Blake had no
formal education but served an apprenticeship
with an engraver. In 1789 he published his
Songs of Innocence, decorated with his own
engravings, then the radical prose work *The
Marriage of Heaven and Hell* (1790) and the *Songs
of Experience* (1794). A great craftsman and a
compulsive worker, Blake wrote verses of
deceptive simplicity and sweetness which
reveal, however, much righteous anger and
fierce idealism.

**CARROLL, Lewis (Charles Lutwidge
Dodgson)**
(1832–1898) UK
Lewis Carroll rapidly became famous for his
two great works of fantasy and distorted logic,
Alice's Adventures in Wonderland (1865) and
Through the Looking-glass (1872), but he was
already celebrated in academic circles as a
lecturer in mathematics at Oxford. Queen
Victoria, expressing her admiration for *Alice*,
asked Carroll for a copy of his next book and
was dismayed to receive a learned tome about
Euclidian geometry.

CARRYL, Charles Edward
(1841–1920) USA
Carryl was a New York businessman who ran
railroad companies in a single-minded manner

until one day he came upon a copy of *Alice's
Adventures in Wonderland*. Inspired by this he
began to write fantasy stories interspersed with
verses for his own children. The best of these
are *Davy and the Goblin* (1886) and *The Admiral's
Caravan* (1892).

CHESTERTON, Gilbert Keith
(1874–1936) UK
Poet, novelist, critic, and artist, Chesterton
was extraordinarily prolific. Among his works
are full-length studies of Dickens, Browning,
Stevenson, and St. Thomas Aquinas. He is
principally famous, however, for the Father
Brown stories. A stubborn and formidable
writer, Chesterton was otherwise renowned for
his bumbling absent-mindedness and his
unfailing ability to get lost.

COWPER, William
(1731–1800) UK
Originally trained as a solicitor, Cowper
disliked the law and gave it up. He wrote
several well-known hymns, some satires, and
the well-known "John Gilpin" (1782), "The
Task" (1784), and short poems such as "To
Mary" (1802). Cowper's style reflects the
simplicity of his nature and marks a transition
from the formal classicism of the eighteenth
century to the freer forms of the nineteenth
century.

DICKINSON, Emily Elizabeth
(1830–1886) USA
The daughter of a wealthy lawyer from
Amherst, Massachusetts, Emily Dickinson lived
the quiet life of a respectable, intellectual
spinster. She had several very intelligent male
friends, but was otherwise a recluse for the last
twenty-five years of her life. No one knew
until she died that she had written more than a
thousand poems of remarkable sensitivity and
originality. Like the English naturalist Gilbert
White, she expressed the sharp, ecstatic pangs
occasioned by everyday things precisely
observed. Her images were eccentric, witty,
and concise.

EMERSON, Ralph Waldo
(1803–1882) USA
Essayist, philosopher, and poet, Emerson was
born in America but came to England in 1833,
meeting Coleridge, Wordsworth (q.v.)
and many other prominent poets. His first
great work, *Nature* (1836), was a philosophical

essay. Many of his early poems appeared in *The Dial*, of which he was editor. His *Essays* were published in 1841 and 1844, his *Poems* in 1847, and his *Journals* from 1909–1914

EWING, Juliana Horatia (née Gatty)
(1841–1885) UK
Daughter of the founder of the successful children's monthly *Aunt Judy's Magazine*, Juliana Ewing rapidly became the magazine's principal contributor of verses and stories. Her best known work is *The Miller's Thumb* (1873), republished as *Jan of the Windmill* (1884).

FIELD, Eugene
(1850–1895) USA
Born in St. Louis, Missouri, Field was a columnist with the *Chicago Morning News*, contributing literary and humorous pieces or light verse. His most well known poem, "Wynken Blynken and Nod", was written in bed "upon brown wrapping paper" one night in March 1889 when the entire poem suddenly came into his head.

HARDY, Thomas
(1840–1928) UK
Initially an architect, poet and novelist Hardy wrote a large number of very popular novels about his native Dorset, including *Tess of the d'Urbevilles* (1891) and *Jude the Obscure* (1895). He regarded fiction, however, merely as a means of making a living, and longed instead to write verse. After the publication of *Jude the Obscure* he gave up novel-writing and devoted the rest of his life to poetry. Although they use conventional forms, Hardy's poems are startlingly original in tone and syntax.

KIPLING, (Joseph) Rudyard
(1865–1936) UK
Born in Bombay and educated in England, Kipling returned to India in 1882 and rapidly acquired a reputation as a brilliant reporter and satirical poet. He settled in London in 1889. His most popular works include *The Jungle Books* (1894 and 5), *Stalky and Co.* (1899), *Kim* (1901), and *Just So Stories* (1902). He was a fine wordsmith; "A word," he said, "should fall in its place like a bell in a full chime."

LEAR, Edward
(1812–1888) UK
Principally known as the father of nonsense verse and chief exponent of the limerick, Lear was also a considerable traveller and so fine a painter that he was invited to teach Queen Victoria to paint in watercolours. His *Book of Nonsense* (1846) was written for the grandchildren of his patron, The Earl of Derby.

LUCAS, Edward Verrall
(1868–1938) UK
Essayist and biographer – and one-time assistant editor of *Punch*, Lucas wrote a biography of Charles Lamb and edited his works and letters. Aside from these, his best-known writing is contained in the light works *The Open Road* (1899) and *The Friendly Town* (1905).

MARVELL, Andrew
(1621–1678) UK
Marvell made his living principally as a private tutor, first to the daughter of Lord Fairfax, then to the son of Oliver Cromwell's ward, William Dutton. In 1657 he became John Milton's assistant and wrote several poems in praise of both Milton and Cromwell. His poems, which include "To His Coy Mistress" and "The Garden," were not published until 1681.

MELVILLE, Herman
(1819–1891) USA
Born in New York, Melville had perhaps the most adventurous life of all the modern writers. A sailor, he served on the whaler *Dolly* and, in 1842, having rounded Cape Horn, abandoned his ship and its brutal captain and sought refuge in the Marquesas Islands. Here he and his friend were held captive by the cannibal tribe, the Typees. He recounted this tale in *Typee, a Peep at Polynesian Life* (1846). His greatest book, however, is the tale of Captain Ahab's obsessive hunt of the great white whale in *Moby Dick* (1851).

RANDS, William Brighty
(1823–1882) UK
Rands was a self-educated children's poet who was born and spent most of his life in or about West London.

RILEY, James Whitcomb
(1849–1916) USA
A Hoosier poet renowned for his absent-minded eccentricity, Riley was born in Greenfield, Indiana and remained forever loyal

to his birthplace. He became one of the United States' best-loved poets, particularly for "Little Orphan Annie" (1886). In 1912 children in schools throughout America celebrated his birthday.

ROSSETTI, Christina Georgina
(1830–1894) UK

Sister of the poet and painter Dante Gabriel Rossetti, Christina led a sad life and failed to fulfill her early exceptional promise. She twice rejected suitors because of her high Anglican religious principles, and her verses are devout and full of the sadness of "what might have been." Her first collection, *Goblin Market* (1862), is her finest, but *Sing-Song* (1872) is full of charming, simple verses for children. She was always frail and, at the time of *Sing-Song*'s composition, was very close to death from Grave's disease. Thereafter she taught with her mother and wrote "morally improving" verse.

THACKERAY, William Makepeace
(1811–1863) UK

Originally a lawyer, then an artist, Thackeray started to contribute pieces to *Punch* in 1842. His finest book, *Vanity Fair*, was published in monthly numbers from 1847 to 1848, then came *The History of Pendennis* (1848–50), *Esmond* (1852), *The Newcomes* (1853–55), and *The Virginians* (1857–59).

THOMPSON, D'Arcy Wentworth
(1829–1902) UK

Thompson was a Classics Master at Edinburgh University, where his pupils included Robert Louis Stevenson. He wrote *Nursery Nonsense or Rhymes without Reason* (1864) for his small son.

WORDSWORTH, William
(1770–1850) UK

The poet laureate lived at Grasmere in the English Lake District with his sister Dorothy. At his best, as in "The Prelude" or "Tintern Abbey," Wordsworth was a brilliant, thoughtful nature poet; at his worst he was capable of gaucheness and banality.

YEATS, William Butler
(1865–1939) Ireland

Born in Dublin, Ireland, Yeats was the guiding genius behind the establishment of the Irish National Theatre Company. Yeats's marvellous lyrical verse and ballads are contained in a host of collections, from *Poems* (1895) to *The Winding Stair* (1933).

THE PAINTERS

INDEX OF FIRST LINES

Other Premier Picturemacs you will enjoy

The Christmas Handbook   Malcolm Bird/Alan Dart
Jack The Treacle Eater   Charles Causley/Charles Keeping
A Second Golden Treasury of Children's Verse   Mark Daniel
A First Treasury of Fairy Tales   Michael Foss
A Second Treasury of Fairy Tales   Michael Foss
Black Beauty   Anna Sewell/Robin McKinley/Susan Jeffers
The Magic Ointment   Eric Quayle/Michael Foreman
The Enchanter's Spell   Gennady Spirin
The Enchanted World Part One   Amabel Williams-Ellis/Moira Kemp
The Enchanted World Part Two   Amabel Williams-Ellis/Moira Kemp

For a complete list of Picturemac and Premier Picturemac titles write to:

Macmillan Children's Books, 18–21 Cavaye Place,
London SW10 9PG